FARM ANIMALS

Rabbits

by Hollie Endres

BELLWETHER MEDIA • MINNEAPOLIS, MN

Note to Librarians, Teachers, and Parents:

Blastoff! Readers are carefully developed by literacy experts and combine standards-based content with developmentally-appropriate text.

Level 1 provides the most support through repetition of high-frequency words, light text, predictable sentence patterns, and strong visual support.

Level 2 offers early readers a bit more challenge through varied simple sentences, increased text load, and less repetition of high frequency words.

Level 3 advances early-fluent readers toward fluency through increased text and concept load, less reliance on visuals, longer sentences, and more literary language.

Level 4 builds reading stamina by providing more text per page, increased use of punctuation, greater variation in sentence patterns, and increasingly challenging vocabulary.

Level 5 encourages readers to move from "learning to read" to "reading to learn" by providing even more text, varied writing styles, and less familiar topics.

Whichever book is right for your reader, Blastoff! Readers are the perfect books to build confidence and encourage a love of reading that will last a lifetime!

This edition first published in 2008 by Bellwether Media.

No part of this publication may be reproduced in whole or in part without written permission of the publisher. For information regarding permission, write to Bellwether Media Inc., Attention: Permissions Department, Post Office Box 1C, Minnetonka, MN 55345-9998.

Library of Congress Cataloging-in-Publication Data
Endres, Hollie J.
  Rabbits / by Hollie J. Endres.
    p. cm. – (Blastoff! readers. Farm animals)
Summary: "A basic introduction to rabbits and how they live on the farm. Simple text and full color photographs. Developed by literacy experts for students in kindergarten through third grade"–Provided by publisher.
  Includes bibliographical references and index.
  ISBN-13: 978-1-60014-085-3 (hardcover : alk. paper)
  ISBN-10: 1-600014-085-8 (hardcover : alk. paper)
  1. Rabbits–Juvenile literature. I. Title.

SF453.2.E53 2008
636.932'2–dc22   2007007465

Contents

Some rabbits live
on farms.
Other rabbits live
in the **wild**.

Rabbits have two
long ears.
These help rabbits
hear very well.

Rabbits have
soft fur.
Most rabbits
have short fur.

Angora rabbits have long fur. Some people make **yarn** from their fur.

Rabbits eat plants.

A rabbit's teeth
can grow long.
Rabbits chew
on things to wear
down their teeth.

15

Most farm rabbits
live in a cage
called a **hutch**.

Rabbits hop around the farmyard to get exercise.

This rabbit needs
to rest.
He's tired.

Glossary

Angora—a kind of rabbit with long, soft hair

hutch—a cage for small animals

wild—living in nature

yarn—thread used for knitting or weaving

To Learn More

AT THE LIBRARY
Ganeri, Anita. *Rabbits*. Chicago, Ill.: Heinemann, 2003.

Schuh, Mari C. *Rabbits on the Farm*. Mankato, Minn.: Capstone Press, 2003.

ON THE WEB
Learning more about farm animals is as easy as 1, 2, 3.

1. Go to www.factsurfer.com

2. Enter "farm animals" into search box.

3. Click the "Surf" button and you will see a list of related web sites.

With factsurfer.com, finding more information is just a click away.

Index

The photographs in this book are reproduced through the courtesy of: Eric Isselee, front cover; Woody Stock, p. 5; SKS, p. 7; Misha Shiyanov, p. 9; Arco Images/Alamy, p. 11; Maximilian Weinzierl/Alamy, p. 13; Woody Stock, p. 15; Arco Images/Alamy, p. 17; PBWPIX/Alamy, p. 19; Andrew Linscott/Alamy, p. 21.